Literature, Literacy, and Learning

 Classroom Teachers, Library Media Specialists, and the Literature-based Curriculum

Eleanor R. Kulleseid and
Dorothy S. Strickland

AMERICAN LIBRARY ASSOCIATION

Chicago and London 1989

Cover designed by Michael Brierton

Text designed by Marcia Lange

Composed by ALA Books on a BestInfo Wave4 pre-press system and output by AnzoGraphics on a Linotronic L300

Printed on 50-pound Glatfelter B-31, a pH-neutral stock, and bound in 10-point Carolina cover stock by First Impression, Inc.

The paper used in this publication meets the minimum requirements of American National Standard for Information Sciences—Permanence of Paper for Printed Library Materials, ANSI Z39.48-1984. ∞

Library of Congress Cataloging-in-Publication Data

Kulleseid, Eleanor R.
   Literature, literacy, and learning : classroom teachers, library
media specialists, and the literature-based curriculum / by Eleanor R.
Kulleseid and Dorothy S. Strickland.
     p.   cm.
  Includes bibliographical references.
  ISBN 0-8389-3376-9
  1. Literature—Study and teaching (Elementary) 2. Reading
(Elementary) 3. Literacy programs. 4. Media programs (Education)
I. Strickland, Dorothy S. II. Title.
LB1575.K8 1989
372.4—dc20   89-27515
                                     CIP

93 92 91 90 89   5 4 3 2 1

Contents

Prologue

Some people there are who, being grown, forget the horrible task of learning to read. It is perhaps the greatest single effort that the human undertakes, and he must do it as a child. . . . . I remember that words—written or printed—were devils, and books, because they gave me pain, were my enemies.[1]

John Steinbeck, the writer of these words, must have been a reluctant reader in his early years. Perhaps his primary grade teachers tried in vain to entice him with "Run, Spot, run." We are fortunate that he was finally lured into a lifetime passion for language and literature, not by Dick and Jane but by an abridged version of Thomas Malory's cycle of Arthurian legends. It was given to him by an aunt, who may have suspected that some magic in the book might awaken the reader's imagination. Near the end of his life Steinbeck returned to childhood literary roots to recreate the story world that had shaped his own life's work. *The Acts of King Arthur and His Noble Knights* is his last gift to a worldwide community of English readers.

How is it that a writer of genius found learning to read and the act of reading so difficult and so unrewarding? To what books had he been exposed before Arthur entered his life? Why were there no Merlins to guide his schooling? These and other related questions have preoccupied the collective minds of parents, educators, politicians, and the business establishment for over a century of rapid growth in American public education. Today, with the emergence of new technologies and profound socioeconomic changes, there is renewed commitment to improving education for all children. There is recognition that literacy—the ability of a person both to read and to write the native language—is the foundation for achievement in the school and the marketplace. There is also a growing realization that the process of literacy acquisition must be pleasurable as well as practical if we are to help children become life-long learners.

The first steps toward literacy are taken when infants learn to differentiate sounds in the environment so that family voices are recognized, and to add their cries, coos, and early words to the human conversation. Listening and speaking are cornerstones for the development of literacy, which takes place over a long period of time with the help of many people: parents, older siblings, teachers, classmates, language arts specialists, and library media specialists. All have something to contribute because, whatever the situation—a reading conference with the teacher, a written entry into a journal, a conversation on the playground or at the dinner table, a bedtime storyreading—they are helping children to use language as a powerful tool to get things done: to express feelings and ideas; to find out what others are thinking and feeling; to learn more about the world;

and for the sheer pleasure and enjoyment of words themselves. Children who understand the functions of spoken language are highly motivated to master reading and writing. Those who understand the speech-print connection are usually ready to make the leap.

In recent years a number of exciting innovations in language arts instruction have been made in response to concerns about a national decline in reading comprehension and writing abilities.[2] Educators have come to believe that children's early experiences with print should be as meaningful and far-ranging as their everyday encounters with spoken language. As a result, school systems across the nation have implemented a number of important changes in their language arts programs, changes which have had a significant effect on the overall curriculum. They are based on approaches that build on what is known about language development, learning, and literature. The California Reading Initiative is one of the first and most fully conceptualized models. "We see the whole movement to improve language arts as incorporating features such as a literature-based curriculum, which means that we systematically, kindergarten through grade twelve, expose our young people to the best of classic and contemporary literature, and we search for meaning using literature as the mechanism. We also believe that. . . the curriculum should not be fragmented, but that we should integrate speaking, listening, reading, and writing."[3]

LITERATURE, LITERACY, AND LEARNING describes theoretical concepts, research findings, and innovative instructional practices that both support and demonstrate successful literature-based literacy programs. The first chapter summarizes theory and research in early language development, writing development, early reading, reading problems, story comprehension, and reader response to literature. The second chapter illustrates the effect of this research on the elementary school curriculum, suggests some promising practices, and presents a vignette of one literature-based language arts program in action. Implications for school library media programs are discussed more fully in the third chapter, which suggests some collaborative processes for introducing, planning, and implementing literature-based programs. Student, parent, teacher, administrator, and library media specialist partnerships are emphasized.

Many of the ideas and practices mentioned in this volume are illustrated in a companion videotape program, *Literature, Literacy, and Learning*, produced by Encyclopaedia Britannica Educational Corporation. The video documents the efforts of educators to introduce and implement innovative literacy programs in elementary school classrooms and library media centers all over the country. Teachers and library media specialists, shown working with students and with one another, reflect upon their efforts to improve students' learning by changing their own practices. Francie Alexander of the California State Department of Education describes the literature-based curriculum model developed in California. Dorothy Strickland summarizes the essential features of good literature-based literacy programs, and teachers, library media specialists, and students demonstrate the use of literature as the springboard for writing, speaking, and thinking activities. These multiple perspectives offer a strong and flexible framework for assessing professional priorities and rethinking the library media professional's contributions to partnerships that foster literacy, learning, and love of literature.

A viewers' guide for the *Literature, Literacy, and Learning* video was prepared by Encyclopaedia Britannica to assist educators in using the video with large and small groups. The complete text for this guide is reprinted as an appendix to this book.

Notes

1. John Steinbeck, Introduction, *The Acts of King Arthur and His Noble Knights, from the Winchester Mss. of Thomas Malory and Other Sources*, ed. Chase Horton (New York: Farrar, Straus & Giroux, 1976), xi.

2. Richard C. Anderson et al., *Becoming a Nation of Readers* (Washington, D.C.: National Institute of Education, 1985).

3. Francie Alexander, interviewed during production of video *Literature, Literacy, and Learning* 1989.

Chapter

1

◆

Literacy Theory and Research

A Common Framework

Teachers and library media specialists who work with young children have always been advocates of literacy and celebrators of literature, well aware of the nourishment a good story brings to mind and heart. Nevertheless, literature appreciation has often been neglected as being beyond the ken of children who have not yet mastered basic skills. Part of the problem is pedagogical; there has never been full agreement on which methods are best for teaching reading and writing. Controversy persists because literacy is the *sine qua non* for learning in all the content areas. Two theoretical poles have been described in a lengthy debate that is often more polemical than analytical.

> At one extreme is a parts-to-whole, sound-symbol-based approach to beginning reading instruction which emphasizes the child's *acquisition* of discrete skills of text decoding. These are taught to the child by the teacher in small, incremental steps, using teacher-selected, controlled vocabulary texts and workbook exercises. Learning is text-centered, and the child reads for the purpose of practice. Reading is taught as a separate activity, in isolation from other subjects.
>
> At the opposite extreme is a holistic, meaning-based approach that emphasizes the child's *use* of a complex array of linguistic skills and competencies already mobilized in the course of learning how to speak. Learning is child- or mind-centered, and the child reads self-selected, unedited whole texts for the purpose of meaning with the teacher's assistance. Reading is taught in concert with other communication acts—speaking, listening, writing—that occur within a social context.[1]

Most practitioners would place themselves towards the middle of the continuum between the two poles. Teachers are usually pragmatists; they do the best they can with the resources that are available to help children learn. They know that the pedagogical pendulum has swung back and forth between the two poles in historic cycles. Nevertheless, there is no question that the teaching of literacy has changed considerably during the past decade, partly because of the increasing numbers of students who are unable or unwilling to read and partly because new research insights into literacy acquisition have

1

led to an expanded repertoire of instructional approaches. The current debate between conservative guardians of the sacred phonics flame and radical basal-burning, whole-language fanatics continues unabated, but there are some signs of compromise.[2] Many practitioners agree that, whatever one's position regarding the teaching of literacy, there are certain shared beliefs that provide a common framework for current curriculum revision. The following is a list of six such beliefs or principles.

1. *Seeking meaning is important.* Learning is active not passive. Students will make the effort to learn to read and write if they are highly motivated; that is, if activities are personally interesting and meaningful to them. This active seeking of meaning, rather than a passive reception of information, is a vital condition for establishing habits of critical thinking and life-long learning.

2. *Oral language development is important for literacy development.* The course of literacy development, including the associated attitudes and skills of reading and writing, is comparable to and interrelated with that of oral language development. Reading, like listening, is receptive; it involves decoding, comprehending, and interpreting print messages created by others. Writing, like speaking, is productive; it involves composing, encoding, and revising print messages to be read by others. All forms of communication require an active learning stance.

3. *Teaching and learning the language arts are best done in an integrated framework.* Reading is best taught as one of four acts of communication that include writing, speaking, and listening, as illustrated in figure 1. All are important to learning; each reinforces the others. Children comprehend and compose oral and textual messages as part of an interrelated language arts curriculum.

4. *Literature is important in integrated language arts programs and should be used across the curriculum.* Much of the content of reading and listening is taken from unedited whole texts that are complex, aesthetically appealing, and interesting to the

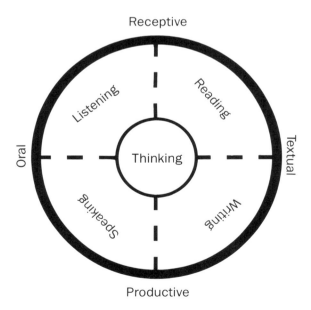

Figure 1. The Language Acts

reader. Such texts present readers with information, ideas, and social values that enrich classroom discourse and learning in all subject areas. Children's literature, both informative and imaginative, provides an enormous and varied resource base for the curriculum.

5. *Varied instructional groupings, approaches, and materials are important for language arts instruction.* Textbook-driven, teacher-directed lectures, lessons, and other whole group instructional activities are no longer the dominant model. Students also work and learn together in pairs and in mixed-ability small groups as well as alone. The teacher may or may not be directly involved. The timeframe is flexible, depending on the nature of a given unit and the capacities of the students involved. The materials used vary, depending on the task and the student, but at least some of the reading matter will be self-selected by students. Although literature is the main reading fare, basal and supplementary readers, workbooks, phonics, and other exercises may also be used in the program. The teacher chooses the materials that are appropriate to the learning situation.

6. *The teacher plays an important role as instructional manager.* The teacher assumes greater responsibility for the management of curriculum: time, sequence, resources, and strategies. The teacher functions in dual capacities as leader and learner; as mentor and monitor; as collaborator and conductor; as sympathetic shoulder and high-wire artist.

This admittedly eclectic framework of educational beliefs has evolved partly from common-sense classroom experience and experimentation, and partly from an important body of research that is summarized below in the following order: early language development, early writing development, early reading, reading problems, story comprehension, and response to literature.

Early Language: Learning to Speak the Native Tongue

Developmental psychologists have produced an enormous and rich body of work from which we have learned much about children's thinking and language acquisition. Early child studies by Vygotsky, Piaget, and others were the foundation for later work by such researchers as Peter and Jill de Villiers, Courtney Cazden, and James Britton.[3]

They have concluded that all children, regardless of country of origin, language group, ethnic or socio-economic background, learn to speak the native tongue in similar ways. It doesn't matter whether we are English teachers or Chinese farmers, street musicians or Wall Street financial analysts. By the time we are five years old, most of us have become fluent speakers, masters of our native languages with a deep intuitive knowledge of grammatical rules: verb tenses, plurals, possessives, negatives, and other complex formal structures. Our vocabularies have probably expanded to include roughly half of any words we will ever use in spoken discourse as adults. How has this mastery been achieved? Here are some features common to successful language acquisition.

> Learning oral language is initiated and controlled by the child. From birth the human brain is programmed to seek for meaning and to organize sensations into coherent mental structures. Children do not merely imitate their elders; they have the innate capacity to construe meaning, to create patterns of speech and thought, and to experiment with them. When researchers examine many of the errors young children make in speech, they discover that children are over-applying a proper rule of grammar to a situation which happens to be an exception. For example, when a child says, "I goed to the library yesterday," he or she is over-applying a rule that works most of the time—add "ed" to an action to make it past tense.

Errors or miscues, as they are often called, give us insight into the child's intuitive thinking and learning strategies.

Mastery of oral language—listening and speaking—is achieved without formal instruction. Learning and practicing language is informal and spontaneous—not taught by adults to the child in structured and sequenced lessons. Adults do model correct and expanded language forms to children when they converse with them and when they read aloud to them from formal texts.

Mastery of oral language is contextualized and purposeful—that is, children listen and learn to speak because they are highly motivated to express feelings, to give and get information, to satisfy social needs, and to use language as an object of play—simply for the fun of it. Structured drill and practice of specific skills are not needed because language is integral to the social, physical, cognitive, and affective contexts within which each child lives. Several researchers have studied the functions or purposes that language serves for children. We may synthesize numerous communicative functions identified by Weeks, Halliday, and others into four broad categories, illustrated with samples of language from two preschool classrooms.[4]

The first is the expressive function, in which language is used to communicate personal feelings, needs, or demands. At the sink, clutching a measuring cup, one child says to another, "I had it first!" At snack time, another exclaims over the cookies, "Oh, those smell yummy!"

A second is the social function, in which language is used to interact with others, and to sustain contact. At lunchtime, a child smiles and says to his table mates, "Guess what? I saw a cookie monster eating a plate." A girl at the water table pouring and making suds, "Look what I'm doing—lookit! Look, Miss Greenbell. I got special cake dessert. C'mere. I'm only gon' give teachers."

The third is the informational function, in which language is used to offer information, and to plan, recall, and interpret experiences. While taking his turn mixing batter, a child muses to no one in particular, "I wonder what the cake is going to look like?" Another child at the art table, dipping her brush into newly introduced white poster paint, comments to the teacher, "This looks like cream. You can't eat it, though, 'cause it's really paint . . . you mix it, like this."

A fourth is the aesthetic function, in which language is used in a playful and imaginative way, communicated as an object of enjoyment and pleasure for its own sake. Three girls are parading around the classroom at snack time, chanting, "We like honey. We like milk. We like juice. We like cookies. . . " (and on and on). And at the art table, the same trio vary a single refrain borrowed from *The Wizard of Oz*, "Ding, dong, the witch is dead.":"Ding, dong, the witch's head." (giggles) "Witch's *head*?" (giggles) "Ding, dong, the witch's bed." (more giggles)

Learning how to listen and speak is interactive; it is largely achieved through social interaction with others, and less through solitary (voluntary) drill and practice. Adults and peers are important teachers, but they do not teach by direct instruction. They model language use, and they stimulate language use through dialogue.

Early Writing: Making the Translation from Speech to Print

Speaking and writing are both productive language activities that involve composing and communicating messages to others or to oneself. Chomsky, Clay, Graves, Temple, and other researchers have observed that many children begin to experiment with writing long before they learn how to read and that writing development parallels that of speech in many ways.[5] Early writing efforts are usually initiated and controlled by the child. Children experiment with language, creating rules and patterns for spelling and grammar, testing them and revising them as maturation and experience increase their knowledge of correct forms. Many children's first written messages include some combination of letters and signs. Just as it takes time for the ear to sort out sentences, phrases, words, and syllables from a stream of speech sounds, it takes time and practice for the eye and hand to transcribe units of meaningful sound into comparable text forms. Even when children have begun to write more fluently, sound-print correspondence takes time to develop.

In the autobiographical sample shown in figure 2, a first grader has grasped some basic print conventions. Her words are written from left to right, and the lines flow from top

Figure 2. Two pages from "The book ubot wen I was a bayby a chaptr book " ("The Book About When I Was a Baby: A Chapter Book."). On the right page, "Chapter 1"; on the left page, "When I was 1 month I was in the hospital. I was very cute. I like the nurse." Anna, grade 1

to bottom of the page. She has also divided phrases and sentences with horizontal lines. Within those blocks her ability to match speech sounds to printed letters is fairly well developed, but words are sometimes run together, as in the third phrase, "I wasvere cyot." She has not yet grasped one basic print convention. Furthermore, the pages of her book are ordered from right to left (back to front) rather than left to right.

Examples of many different types of written communication (letters, labels, books, newspapers, charts, etc.) are usually found in home and school environments in which early writing occurs. Children are motivated to write because it fulfills personal needs. Writing is purposeful and serves a number of important functions that are the same as those identified above for speech: expressive, social, informational, and aesthetic functions. It takes time for young writers to move from so-called invented, or transitional, spelling patterns into standard ones. Correct alphabetic forms of spelling and syntax are not easily learned through direct teaching in the early stages of writing development. Children's learning is informal; improvement comes more with maturation and practice than with systematic early instruction. Thus early experiences with writing, like those of oral language, involve an intuitive rather than systematic application of rules and speech patterns.

On the other hand, standard forms are not neglected. Once children begin to recognize word patterns and begin to read phrases, they become more aware of standard spelling forms and wish to emulate them in their original written work. Most writing process curricula for the early grades include opportunities to write a first draft, revise the draft, and publish it as a completed book, usually for the classroom or school library media center. Teachers have different expectations and procedures for these activities, depending on the child and group. However, in most situations, for a book to be published and placed with other published print works, the revised final version is cast in standard English. Children who are learning to read understand that standard spelling and grammatical forms facilitate comprehension. They want others to read and enjoy their writing.

After writing and illustrating the first draft of his "Book About the Boat (figure 3A)," a six-year-old was asked to circle the words that he needed to have spelled correctly for the final published version. After they were added to his word list, he revised the story. On the page shown in figure 3B, he corrected the spelling and added more detail to the illustration, making it clearer that the boy is standing on a dock after the boat has been moored.

A number of studies have commented on the effect of microcomputers and word processing programs on the frequency and fluency of writing in the middle grades. Computers facilitate editing and revision; children are relieved from the burden of correcting by rewriting whole texts by hand. There is no question that, under the appropriate circumstances, computers in the classroom can be used to facilitate the composing, revising, and editing process for young authors.[6]

Early Reading

There is a considerable body of research dealing with children who learn to read fluently without formal instruction at home and before formal instruction is begun in kindergarten and first grade. Durkin, Clark, and others have documented some of the characteristics such children share in common.[7]

Early readers are read aloud to on a regular basis at home. They have early and frequent exposure to books, reading, print, and pictures of all kinds. Adult readers model

Figure 3A. Page from first draft

reading behaviors and expose children to unedited stories cast in formal book language that presents complex semantic and syntactical forms. Familiarity with narrative story structure helps children organize their own experiences into coherent verbal structures and to make sense of new texts when they are encountered.

Early readers have opportunities to talk about books, reading, print, and illustrations with adult readers. Parents will often encourage children to tell the story with them or may ask questions about the story. As the story is repeated in future tellings, it becomes a vehicle for social interaction and an object for reflection. The child becomes a co-reader, a construer of meaning in a pleasurable and informal situation. Educators have studied and tried to replicate these home lap-reading situations in school because they appear to have powerful impact on children's literacy development.

Early readers have opportunities to choose books they want to hear or browse through. They may select from a range of books available in the home and/or borrowed from a community library. This process of self-selection is often initiated when an adult reader/translator is unavailable and the child is motivated to repeat a pleasurable experience. Opportunity and desire to choose a book seem to be extremely important in establishing children's positive orientation to literacy.

I was scared becduse it was dark.

Figure 3B. Published version of written narrative. Xai Xing, grade 1

Linguistic and Cultural Diversity

Young children who have difficulties learning how to read after being exposed to systematic instruction in school may have biologically or psychologically based learning problems. They may also come from homes where reading has not been an important part of family life. They may come from homes in which the spoken language is either an English dialect or a different language altogether. Educators often label such children as culturally disadvantaged as well as learning disabled.

The study and remediation of learning disabilities has been a major thrust of the educational research agenda for many years. Clinical studies have supported a rapidly growing special education field in which more and more children have been diagnosed as learning or developmentally disabled. One disturbing trend has been the high number of children from dialect or bilingual backgrounds who are labeled in this way. There has been a growing concern about the assumptions underlying such diagnoses, leading to recognition that if Johnny can't read or write, the problem may lie not so much in perceived deficits as in actual differences between home and school cultures. Now, thanks to landmark ethnographic studies, which compare school with home environments, educators know more about the linguistic strengths and attitudes that children bring to the school situation. When educators think in terms of cultural diversity rather than cultural disadvantage, they are able to plan and implement programs that offer different ways of introducing mainstream functional literacy to all children.[8]

A number of such studies center on classrooms and schools in which teachers are struggling to introduce literacy to heterogeneous populations with different class, ethnic, cultural, and linguistic backgrounds. Shirley Brice Heath's landmark study during the seventies documents language acquisition and socialization of children in two southern rural communities—one, black working-class, the other white working-class—analyzing the oral and literate communication mores of each community.[9] Teachers in recently desegregated classrooms use these insights to evaluate and modify their curricula to deal more effectively with the lack of congruence between home dialects and language traditions and the mainstream literacy tradition of the townspeople and school community. Throughout the process, teaching/learning problems are reinterpreted by teachers as cultural communication barriers rather than cultural or cognitive deficiencies in the children. The strategies they develop include a mix of speech and print activities that focus on comparative study of children's language styles as a major part of the language arts curriculum. The outcomes are greater respect for individual and cultural differences as well as understanding and mastery of both home speech and standard English language forms.[10]

Don Holdaway's research has come out of a similar phenomenon, the influx of immigrant Maori and Polynesian families into a relatively large urban school system in Auckland, New Zealand. These children come from home environments in which literacy is not modelled or practiced. Holdaway and his colleagues have taken a different approach to cultural differences, partly because they are working in a multilingual situation, not just with variant dialects of English. By introducing successful mainstream practices to early childhood classrooms, they hope to enculturate children to literacy in English. In the "shared book experience," big books are used with a heterogeneous group of children to emulate successful home lap reading that promotes literacy for individual children from mainstream environments. Holdaway's paradigm for emergent literacy includes group listening and looking at stories, talking about stories—discussing and sharing story ideas and responses; repetition of stories, and, ultimately, voluntary independent reading of stories by individual children.[11]

Story Comprehension

A significant problem for educators has been the growing amount of evidence that the ability to read does not necessarily ensure understanding or improve comprehension. That is, a child may successfully decode a text, read it aloud perfectly, and not have the faintest idea what it means. This concern, reinforced by a reported steady decline in reading comprehension scores in the middle and upper grades, is reflected in the large body of literature devoted to research on reading comprehension.[12]

Although many research studies evaluate children's comprehension of essay or nonfiction information texts, a growing number focus on children's comprehension of narrative story forms. One assumption is that good stories have certain common structural elements that may be generalized as story grammar. The child's ability to comprehend and remember a story is related to the number of elements or conventions he or she is able to recall when asked to retell the story. Researchers select and adapt a children's story, usually coding significant phrases or events. The story is then told to a sample of children, usually of different ages, and they are asked to retell it to the researcher at various intervals after the initial hearing. Figures 4 and 5 illustrate a story grammar treatment for a folk tale, which has been adapted for testing purposes. In figure 4 each significant phrase is separately numbered; in figure 5 the numbers have been applied to a diagram of story categories or formal elements.

1	Once there was a woman who lived with her husband in the woods.
2	One day, her husband got very sick.
3	The woman was very upset by her husband's illness
4	and wanted him to get well.
5	She tried everything she could think of
6	but nothing worked.
7	At last she remembered that medicine made from a tiger's whisker would help him get well.
8	So the woman set out to get a tiger's whisker.
9	She went to a tiger's cave and put some food in front of the opening to the cave and sang soft music.
10	The tiger came out, ate the food, and thanked the woman for the food and music.
11	The woman quickly cut off one of his whiskers
12	and ran home.
13	The tiger was lonely and sad,
14	but the woman's husband got well.

This is a condensed version of "The Tiger's Whisker" used by Stein and Glenn (1979).

Reprinted with permission of Jill Fitzgerald and the International Reading Association, from "Story Grammars and Reading Instruction," by Jill Fitzgerald Whaley, in *The Reading Teacher* 34 (April 1981); 765.

Figure 4. "The Tiger's Whisker"

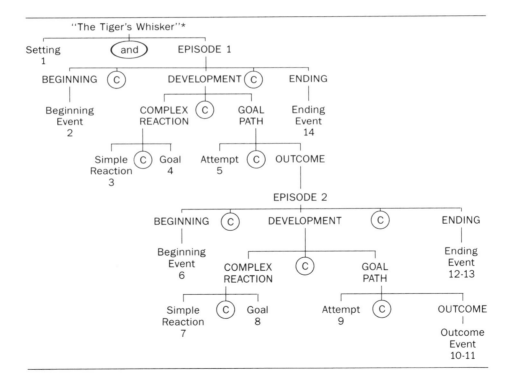

Reprinted with permission of Jill Fitzgerald and the International Reading Association, from "Story Grammars and Reading Instruction," by Jill Fitzgerald Whaley, in *The Reading Teacher* 34 (April 1981): 765.

Figure 5. Identification of the Story Categories for "The Tiger's Whisker"

Lovers of literature might well wonder what kind of experience children are having with a story that has been stripped of colorful language or dialogue to reveal the skeleton. Nevertheless, research of this kind does help to build a developmental continuum of the child's increasing comprehension and recall of narrative discourse, and supports the notion that stories and story-sharing are good learning experiences. It also validates much of the practical wisdom held by story-reading teachers and library media specialists—that even very young children seem to be able to internalize, recall, and use some formal elements of story grammar (beginnings, outcomes, some episodes) in their own narratives.

Another group of related research studies has demonstrated the positive effect of story retellings on children's memory and comprehension.[13] Such retellings often occur spontaneously in young children's dramatic play, in conversations, in their efforts to independently "read" a favorite picture book when an adult isn't available, and in their original writings. Figure 6 shows a kindergartener's reconstruction of a beloved story, created during writers workshop sessions in her classroom. The main characters and key events are presented in proper sequence with simple and direct language, accompanied by expressive drawings. Dialogue, description, figurative language, explanations of cause and effect, characters' states of mind and intentions are omitted, although the illustrations contribute a good deal to the story's impact.

In another type of study, children are asked to create original dictated or written stories. These writing examples are analyzed to identify either internal psychological states or to trace the development of story schema, a term used by cognitive psychologists to identify the child's internal conception of story structure, or how a story should go.[14] Adults are invariably surprised by the content and complexity of young children's thinking as revealed in such stories.

In the example below a five-year-old storyteller has translated his school experiences into powerful and amusing metaphors for learning. This child is metacognitively aware—he is thinking about thinking—but he is expressing his thoughts in a story that has extraordinary aesthetic and emotional dimensions.

> There was a boy named Johnny Hong Kong and finally he grew up and went to school and after that all he ever did was sit all day and think. He hardly even went to the bathroom. And he thought everyday and every thought he thought up his head got bigger and bigger. One day it got so big he had to go live up in the attic with trunks and winter clothes. So his mother bought some gold fish and let them live in his head—he swallowed them—and every time he thought, a fish would eat it up until he was even so he never thought again, and he felt much better.[15]

The narrative form of discourse serves him well in making sense of his own sense-making efforts. This and numerous other original stories amply support the assumption that children need to use narrative as well as expository forms to make sense of the world, and that exposure to such forms increases their ability to use language meaningfully—to comprehend, to interpret, and to communicate ideas. Students who tell one another about last night's episode of a favorite TV series, who turn the doll corner into a space ship and take off for Mars, or who dramatize *Sir Gawain and the Green Knight* for the school assembly are powerful makers of story. There is a wealth of literature in their spontaneous dramatic play scenarios,[16] and in their dictated oral narratives and written stories.[17] Research suggests that such activities provide a child-based context for the acquisition of literacy and should be continued throughout the middle grades both to develop and to evaluate reading comprehension.[18]

Figure 6. "Cindrala" ("Cinderella"). Sarah, grade 2

Figure 6 (cont.) "Cindrala"

Figure 6 (cont.) "Cindrala"

Response to Literature

Story comprehension is closely related to reader response theory, which suggests that reading is a reciprocal interplay between reader and text, or between listener and narrative voice. Louise M. Rosenblatt and Arthur Applebee define two basic approaches to making sense of a text.[19] One is logical, objective, and practical; the reader is interested in abstracting information, analyzing the text for specific meanings for a given purpose. This approach is the efferent (Rosenblatt) or transactional (Applebee) stance, which may be invoked for finding a recipe, scanning the newspaper, or reading this book. The second approach is intuitive, subjective, meditative, even playful; the reader is interested in enjoying the text, in experiencing it as a whole rather than understanding each of its parts. This poetic (Applebee) or aesthetic (Rosenblatt) stance is invoked when the reader is seeking pleasurable engagement with the text, attaching private and personal meanings and appreciating its sensuous qualities. Such an experience is invoked usually by interaction with a literary form—novel, short story, or poem—but can be aroused by contact with expository forms such as the scientific essays of Stephen Jay Gould or Thomas Lewis, works that arouse unexpected delight and emotion because of felicitous expression and powerful ideas.

The importance of both approaches is acknowledged by researchers and practitioners alike, but most would agree that traditional classroom instruction favors the efferent or transactional stance. Texts are chosen for the purpose of conveying information in a clear and systematic way, and reading is focused on accessing that information. The opportunities for experiencing text aesthetically seem to diminish as children grow into the upper grades, as demands increase for reading in the content areas.

Petrosky's query is typical of the questions raised by reader response theorists in evaluating the limits of traditional reading programs. "Does our research tell us that children respond literally within the constraints of concrete operational thinking at ages seven to eleven because this is what children can do, or do they respond literally because we teach them, through years of schooling, to respond within these constraints by emphasizing literal comprehension, paraphrasing, and summarizing?"[20]

Rosenblatt, Vandergrift, and others argue for increasing aesthetic reading experiences, for developing informal strategies to elicit student responses, and for extending such encounters with literature well into the upper grades.[21] The pleasure of literacy can facilitate the business of literacy; attention to personal motivation and aesthetic appreciation seems to have positive consequences for cognitive achievement and textual comprehension.

Literacy research covers a wide range of topics, including early speaking, writing, and reading development, as well as linguistic and cultural diversity, story comprehension, and reader-response theory. However, the summary in this chapter represents only the tip of the iceberg, a metaphor that aptly infers a depth of material available to practitioners who wish to explore these topics further. This important research has provided a foundation for a number of changes in both curriculum content and instructional methods.

Curriculum Trends: Theory into Practice

What changes have occurred in curriculum and instruction as a result of literacy research? The next chapter describes exciting programs that illustrate innovative practices found in classrooms across the nation. Trends influencing these practices include: introducing writing into the curriculum simultaneously with, and even before, reading instruction; developing literacy activities in which speaking and listening occur within the context of child-directed social interaction rather than exclusively teacher-directed responses to questions; more shared reading aloud of trade texts and students' writings, stressing the importance of speaking and listening to an author's voice, translating from print back to speech; teaching comprehension through group discussions, reflecting upon texts and developing shared interpretations of content, rather than merely testing comprehension through written tests, retellings, or summaries; greater and earlier exposure to more complex fiction literature and nonfiction essays through use of unadapted texts found in trade books and, more recently, in some basal reading series; flexible groupings, flexible scheduling of reading activities, individualized and small group use of different texts, and greater freedom of book choice; greater emphasis on the pleasurable, playful, and aesthetic aspects of language and literature; integrating language arts across the content areas of the curriculum so that they function as communication vehicles for learning social studies, science, math, etc., rather than as subjects of separate study; relating literature to other content areas of the curriculum; and seeing narratives as important sources both of cultural information and of social values. These trends will continue to have long-term effect on elementary school students, teachers, administrators, parents, teacher educators, and researchers well into the next century.

Literature-based programs are being implemented throughout the country in a variety of ways. They require different resources and strategies and are directed at different types of student populations. There is no single "correct" model; yet, such programs share many of the characteristics described earlier in the common framework of beliefs about the teaching of literacy. Teachers must assess their current programs and, in a collaborative effort with others in the school community, decide how and when desired changes in the language arts curriculum are to take place. These changes will require them to take risks and try on new roles in the classroom. They will need to help students take more responsibility for their own learning, and they will need to experiment with alternative ways of assessing that learning takes place in their classrooms.

Library media specialists will also need to continue to assess their roles as resource providers, teachers, and instructional consultants, keeping in mind that literature-based literacy programs should provide opportunities for increasing program relevance and visibility. Ken Haycock puts it in the form of a challenge when he states, "Library media specialists are being given their last opportunity to shed isolated instruction as a unitary teacher and to move to a central position on the team . . . as a teaching partner."[22] It is an opportunity to make a powerful case for strong library media collections, programs, and qualified personnel at the elementary level. The second chapter further elaborates the translation of literacy theory into language arts practice by describing teachers and children at work in one literature-based classroom and by sketching vignettes of other programs that illustrate some of the conditions necessary for successful literature-based curricula.

Teachers, principals, library media specialists, reading specialists, and others who have planned and implemented programs such as those described belong to a community of readers, writers, speakers, listeners, and thinkers that excludes no one. Students who learn along with these professionals are fortunate, indeed.

Notes

1. Eleanor R. Kulleseid, "Whole Language and Library Media Programs," *School Library Media Annual 1988*, vol. 6, ed. Jane Bandy Smith (Littleton, Colo.: Libraries Unlimited, 1988), 4.

2. For a recent attempt to reconcile philosophical differences, see reading specialist Carla R. Haymsfeld's "Filling the Hole in Whole Language," *Educational Leadership* 46 (March 1989): 65–68.

3. Jill and Peter de Villiers summarize their research and that of others in *Early Language* (Cambridge, Mass.: Harvard University Press, 1979) and in a video entitled *Out of the Mouths of Babes: The Acquisition of Language*, produced by the Canadian Broadcasting Corp. (New York: Filmmakers Library, [n.d.]). See also Courtney B. Cazden, ed., *Language in Early Childhood Education* (Washington, D.C.: National Association for the Education of Young Children, 1981) and James Britton, *Language and Learning* (London: Penguin, 1970).

4. Thelma E. Weeks, *Born to Talk* (Rowley, Mass.: Newbury House, 1979); Michael A. K. Halliday, *Explorations in the Functions of Language* (London: Edward Arnold, 1973). Language samples were transcribed from a 1984 videotape of preschool classrooms at a private independent school and a day care center in New York City.

5. Carol Chomsky, "Write Now, Read Later," in Cazden, *Language in Early Childhood Education*, 141–149; Lucy M. Calkins, *The Art of Teaching Writing* (Exeter, N.H.: Heinemann, 1986); Marie M. Clay, *What Did I Write?* (Exeter, N.H.: Heinemann, 1975); Donald H. Graves, *Writing: Teachers and Children at Work* (Exeter, N.H.: Heinemann, 1982); Charles A. Temple et al., *The Beginnings of Writing*, 2d ed. (Boston: Allyn and Bacon, 1988).

6. Dorothy S. Strickland et al., *Using Computers in the Teaching of Reading* (New York: Teachers College Press, 1987).

7. Margaret M. Clark, "Literacy at Home and at School: Insights from a Study of Young Fluent Readers," in *Awakening to Literacy*, ed. Hillel Goelman, Antoinette Oberg, and Frank Smith (Portsmouth, N.H.: Heinemann, 1984), 122–130; Delores Durkin, *Children Who Read Early* (New York: Teachers College Press, 1966).

8. Donna M. Gollnick and Philip C. Chinn, "Language," *Multicultural Education in a Pluralistic Society* (St. Louis, Mo.: C. V. Mosby, 1983), 106–136.

9. Shirley Brice Heath, *Ways with Words: Language, Life, and Work in Communities and Classrooms* (London: Cambridge University Press, 1983).

10. Sarah Michaels, " 'Sharing Time': Children's Narrative Styles and Differential Access to Literacy," *Language in Society* 10 (1980): 423–442.

11. Don Holdaway, *The Foundations of Literacy* (New York: Ashton Scholastic, 1979). See also his "Shared Book Experience: Teaching Reading Using Favorite Books," *Theory into Practice* 21 (Autumn 1982): 293–300.

12. For a summary, see Robert J. Tierney and James W. Cunningham, "Research on Teaching Reading Comprehension," *Handbook of Reading Research*, ed. P. David Pearson (New York: Longman, 1984), 609–656.

Mandel Morrow, "Retelling Stories: A Strategy for Improving Young Children's Comprehension, Concept of Story Structure, and Oral Language Complexity," *The Elementary School Journal* 85 (1985): 647–661.

14. Evelyn Goodenough Pitcher and Ernst Prelinger, *Children Tell Stories: An Analysis of Fantasy* (New York: International University Press, 1963); Arthur N. Applebee, *The Child's Concept of Story: Ages Two to Seventeen* (Chicago: University of Chicago Press, 1978); Brian Sutton-Smith et al., *The Folkstories of Children* (Philadelphia: University of Pennsylvania Press, 1981).

15. Pitcher and Prelinger, *Children Tell Stories*, 133.

16. Vivian Gussin Paley, *Bad Guys Don't Have Birthdays* (Chicago: University of Chicago Press, 1988) and *Boys and Girls: Superheroes in the Doll Corner* (Chicago: University of Chicago Press, 1984).

17. Temple et al., *The Beginnings of Writing*. See especially "Part Three: The Beginnings of Composition," 117–258.

18. Gary Zingher's *At the Pirate Academy: Adventures with Language in the Library* (Chicago: American Library Association, forthcoming) describes scenarios for thematic exploring that include story dramatization activities for middle and upper graders.

19. Louise M. Rosenblatt, "The Literary Transaction: Evocation and Response," *Theory into Practice* 21 (Autumn 1982): 268–277, and *The Reader, the Text, the Poem: The Transactional Theory of the Literary Work* (Carbondale: Southern Illinois University Press, 1978); Arthur Applebee, "The Uses of Language," *The Child's Concept of Story*, 10–27.

20. Anthony R. Petrosky, "The Inferences We Make: Children and Literature," *Language Arts* 57 (February 1980): 149–156.

21. Kay E. Vandergrift, *Child and Story: The Literary Connection* (New York: Neal-Schuman, 1980).

22. Ken Haycock, "Whole Language Issues and Implications," *School Library Media Annual 1988*, vol. 6, ed. Jane Bandy Smith.

The Literature-based Curriculum

The concept of the literature-based curriculum is innovative, flexible, and inclusive of many approaches. The process of incorporating children's imaginative and informational literature into the day-to-day curriculum takes place over a period of time and may assume different forms, depending upon teachers' backgrounds, administrative leadership, educational philosophy, goals and objectives and, of course, available resources. A look at state and district curriculum guides shows a considerable diversity in ways literature is integrated into the curriculum at the elementary level. Huck describes three main types of programs.[1] One is the "pure" literature-based literacy or reading program, in which the primary sources for literacy activities are trade children's books. Different types of text structures or literary genre are also read, discussed, and used as models for students' creative writing.

The second type of program is a modified hybrid that uses basal readers flexibly with children's literature. Many of the elements of a literature-based literacy program, such as read-aloud sessions and independent silent reading periods, may be adopted. In addition, many of the newer basal reading series incorporate quality children's literature texts with fewer editorial changes. Teachers who use these basals will integrate more and more children's literature into their curriculum, especially if opportunities and partnerships with supportive library media specialists have been established.

A third type of program introduces children's literature as a separate area of study, usually in the middle and upper grades. In this approach the materials are studied as cultural artifacts. Literary texts, usually organized by genre, are interpreted and analyzed for structure, themes, style, mood, and other literary elements. For example, in a study of poetry students examine different verse forms, meters, and rhyme schemes, while in a study of fiction they would focus on plot, setting, themes, and characters, perhaps distinguishing between historical and modern realistic fiction or between realistic fiction and fantasy. Such programs tend to view the study of literature as a vehicle for exploring cultural values. "The great works in our literary canon reveal the noblest aspirations of the human spirit. They confront students with existential dilemmas that encourage the students' moral and ethical growth. They instruct even as they entertain."[2]

Textual interpretation and reader response, often through discussion, are elements common to literature programs and to literature-based literacy programs. There may be considerable overlap between programs or even the co-existence of more than one approach. For example, California's *Handbook for Planning an Effective Literature Program, Kindergarten through Grade Twelve* "maintains that literature provides the best vehicle possible for teaching all the language arts: reading, listening, speaking, and writing. At the same time, literature is also tremendously valuable for its own sake."[3]

Significant confusion exists about the boundaries of any one of the three basic types of literature programs. In a number of elementary schools the three types of programs co-exist peacefully in individual classrooms. Whatever the curricular circumstances, teachers moving from textbook-centered instruction to a more theme-centered, literature-based approach take on new ways of thinking about teaching and learning. Although they may not be abandoning textbooks and other materials expressly designed for instructional purposes, they are taking greater control over their use. Daily plan books no longer simply list the textbooks and page numbers to be "covered" each day. More likely, the daily plan will involve large chunks of time with varied purposes, materials, and activities taking place concurrently. Themes and projects tie activities together. Subject matter disciplines are less discrete, with many reading, writing, and oral language activities engaged in throughout the day. Literature of all types is used in conjunction with textbooks. Classroom libraries and library media centers include abundant and ever-changing resources. Collections reflect the interests and diverse abilities of the children using them.

Teachers and students take shared responsibility for planning and carrying out learning activities; their objectives determine the materials they use—not the other way around. The overriding goal is for all individuals in each school and in each classroom to function as a community of readers and writers. The overriding challenge for practitioners is to determine and implement the specific steps that will lead them, day by day, week by week, towards that goal.

A Visit to a Literature-based Classroom

For JoAnn Hart and many teachers like her, building a community of readers and writers is no easy task. Setting goals, selecting materials, and organizing and managing the day is an immense challenge. JoAnn is a fourth-grade teacher who, for many years, thought of her reading program primarily in terms of the basal reader prescribed by the district. Like so many teachers, JoAnn taught reading during a separate block of time in which students were given numerous workbook pages and worksheets to keep them occupied while she worked with each of her three reading groups. The language arts textbook was covered meticulously, from cover to cover, whether students needed a particular skill or not. Social studies and science were generally kept separate from other aspects of the curriculum. Each subject area had its own time slots during the week, and each was largely dominated by the textbook purchased for it.

Today, JoAnn is attempting to move toward a more literature-based approach. Textbooks still play a major role in her classroom; however, they are now viewed as one of many important resources rather than the core of the curriculum. Both in the language arts and content areas, children's literature has assumed an expanded and major role. A visit to her classroom reveals how she has managed to link a variety of literary experiences into a web of significant language learning possibilities.

Observations

JoAnn looked up from the journal. Martin was entering the room.

"Good morning Mrs. Hart."

"Good morning Martin," replied JoAnn. She finished the sentence she was writing, closed the journal, and walked to the door to greet the other members of her fourth-grade class. One by one they entered. Most exchanged a word or two with her. A gleeful comment about a book having been completed, a brief progress report on a new baby sister, the proud display of a new birthday sweater, an excuse for not remembering an exercise that was due the day before.

Inside the classroom, children chat informally as they take out their journals and leaf through them to find the first blank page. Gradually everyone settles down to write. For the next ten minutes or so the children write as JoAnn circulates around the room, answering questions, offering assistance, and sometimes responding in writing on the spot. Most often the children simply write about anything that interests them. At other times JoAnn focuses their entries by putting a prompt on the board. They might be asked to reflect on three important things they have learned so far about the solar system or two things that really make a book good. Small-group sharing sessions focused on journal writing generally follow, during which children share and discuss their entries. At times the small groups are asked to reach consensus in order to formulate a list of ideas to be shared with the entire class. Sometimes JoAnn spends journal time simply writing in her own journal, serving as an adult model of an important activity.

The time immediately following the journal writing is spent on announcements and planning for the remainder of the morning. Most of the planning is centered around the large block of time known as their reading/writing workshop. During the planning children are reminded of the various kinds of independent activities that need to be done while JoAnn is engaged with individuals and small groups. The independent activities have been divided into "musts" and "optionals." The activities reflect the child's reading group and frequently differ among the individuals within each group.

"Must" activities often relate to the follow-up work to a basal reader lesson and to the minimum of fifteen minutes of reading in a self-selected book required each day. Each child must have a book from the library media center on hand at all times. Most read at least a chapter a day in school.

At times a science or social studies center-based activity may be a "must" for certain designated children. These activities may require the replication of a science experiment or a mathematical task that JoAnn has demonstrated and wants each child to experience first hand. A few children will be slated for these centers each day. JoAnn sees to it that each center task involves reading directions and note taking of some type. Often, two or three children may work collaboratively on these tasks.

"Optional" activities often relate to long-term tasks such as working on a piece in their writing folders or continuing work on science and social studies projects. Although other specific times are allotted for these purposes, children are encouraged to make use of the reading/writing workshop as well. Long-term projects may involve work in the library media center and the classroom. Because the library media staff is familiar with the topics under study in each classroom, the library media center provides a key source of support for research and content area projects.

During planning time JoAnn requires each child to develop a personal checklist of things to do. Specialized items such as Sofia's trip to the nurse at 10:30 A.M. and Roy's session with the speech teacher at 9:15 A.M. are added to their personal checklists. Those children who are slated for personalized reading conferences write that on their checklists so that they can be ready when JoAnn calls them. The children soon learn to use a kind of shorthand to get their checklists written in a hurry. The idea for the checklists came to JoAnn as she attempted to diversify and personalize her assignments while, at the same time, giving children more responsibility for organizing their day. She soon learned that she had to go beyond good classroom organization and a well planned, predictable day to offer her students some simple personal organizers so that they could gain a sense of control over what was expected of them and free her to work with small groups and individuals.

The reading/writing workshop often begins with a mini-lesson. These are brief, direct instruction activities that may take many forms. They may be used to help children become more sensitive to the writer's craft. For example, one day JoAnn selected stories from the three basal readers currently in use and read aloud descriptive passages from each. The stories were all written by noted authors. The children discussed how interesting and provocative language was used to paint vivid word pictures for the reader. They discussed how writers sometimes used wording to make the reader see, touch, taste, feel, and hear the character's experience. The students were encouraged to try some of these techniques in their own writing. Not all of the mini-lessons focus on the writer's craft. They may focus on the mechanics of writing or on listening, speaking, or study skills. For these lessons JoAnn frequently turns to the language arts textbook and selects a lesson that suits the children's needs. The follow-up activity to these lessons is usually a "must" for everyone.

After the mini-lesson JoAnn begins her work with small groups while the remainder of the class works independently. Interspersed among the small group sessions are a number of personalized reading conferences. The names of those children who will be called for personalized conferences are listed on the board in the morning. The conferences focus on the trade books children are reading independently. The conference takes approximately five minutes and begins with questions and discussion. JoAnn asks a very general question about the book. Obviously she has not read every book the students have selected. She might ask: Why did you select this book? How does this book compare with other mystery stories you have read or other books read by the same author? What is the most exciting part so far? Next, the child selects a brief portion of the book to read aloud. Children like this read-aloud time because it is authentic. After the reading JoAnn turns to the page in her reading conference notebook headed by that child's name. She writes in the date, the title of the book, the page number the child is on, and any observations she might wish to make related to the conference. She tries to get to five or six such conferences each day, assuring each of her 26 students at least one conference per week. (See figure 7.)

JoAnn looks at the clock. It is 10:45. Time to wind up the reading/writing workshop and get ready for a snack and game. If it's a nice day, they'll go outdoors. Everyone scurries about, checking their checklists, tidying up, looking around to see what else needs to be done. They have spent nearly an hour and forty-five minutes in their reading/writing workshop. Yet, the observation has revealed only a few of the ways that this skillful teacher manages to tailor a variety of methods and materials to a holistic framework for learning—a framework that is far different from the typical language arts instruction that dominates so many elementary classrooms.

Reflections

Why are the language arts so effectively integrated in this classroom? The answer centers

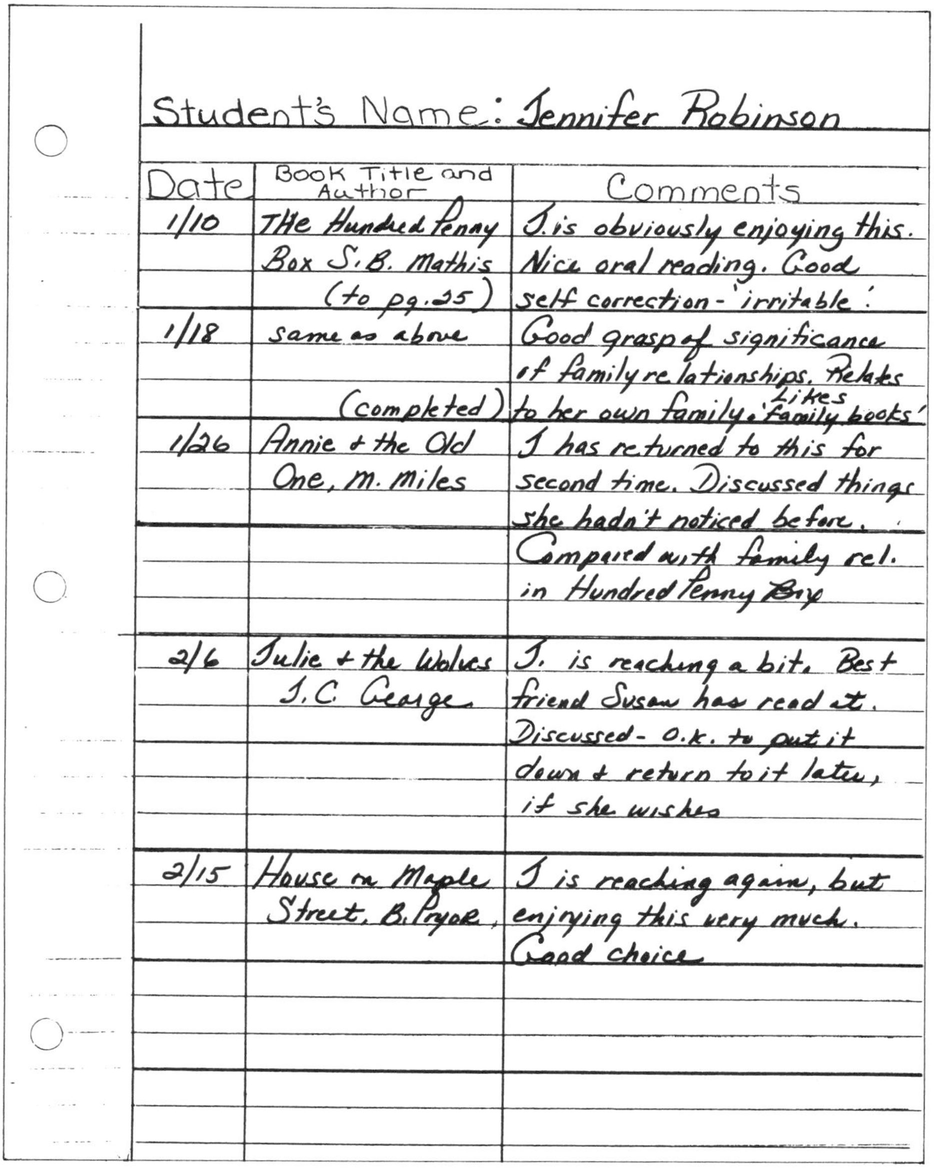

Student's Name: Jennifer Robinson

Date	Book Title and Author	Comments
1/10	The Hundred Penny Box S.B. Mathis (to pg. 25)	J. is obviously enjoying this. Nice oral reading. Good self correction - 'irritable.'
1/18	same as above (completed)	Good grasp of significance of family relationships. Relates to her own family. Likes 'family books'
1/26	Annie & the Old One, M. Miles	J has returned to this for second time. Discussed things she hadn't noticed before. Compared with family rel. in Hundred Penny Box
2/6	Julie & the Wolves J.C. George	J. is reaching a bit. Best friend Susan has read it. Discussed - o.k. to put it down & return to it later, if she wishes
2/15	House on Maple Street, B. Pryor	J is reaching again, but enjoying this very much. Good choice

Figure 7. Sample Reading Conference Notebook

on a set of factors relating to classroom management and to the wide variety of language opportunities shown in figure 8.

Restructuring her approach to reading and the other language arts from a strictly basal orientation to an integrated workshop was a major breakthrough for JoAnn. Its success encouraged her to extend this holistic approach to other aspects of the day and to expand the use of literature. For example, reading aloud is no longer scheduled at the end of the day, to take place only "if time allows." It occurs every day just after lunch break, a

Factors	Characteristics
Classroom management	well organized; predictable; shared planning; shared responsibility; varied organization: whole group, small group, individualized, center-based; varied method: direct teaching, independent activities, cooperative learning.
Opportunities for reading	in journals; in trade books, in language arts and reading texts; for social studies and science projects; during center-based tasks.
Opportunities for writing	in journals (in some cases, written dialogues); free writing, for follow-up activities to direct language arts instruction; for science and social studies projects; for center-based tasks.
Opportunities for listening and speaking	during whole group planning, sharing, and discussion; during small group sharing and discussion; during personalized conversations with teacher; during direct instruction of lessons in listening and speaking.

Figure 8. Planning Learning Experiences in a Literature-based Curriculum

prime time of the day. The read-aloud selection often leads to a variety of types of response, from discussion to art, drama, and writing. Read-aloud selections often relate to social studies and science topics under study. Even books about math and computers have become treasured resources for inquiry and discussion. Sometimes the class focuses on a particular genre or author over a period of time. JoAnn always attempts to help students link the read-aloud selections to their personal reading and writing.

A very important feature of each day is "share time," when students share their personal reading and writing and participate in discussion groups. These share sessions are particularly effective because the student presenter rather than JoAnn leads the discussion. JoAnn admits that it took considerable time and effort for her to resist monopolizing the talk with her own agenda. She is amazed and gratified as she observes students talk as evidence of their growing confidence and competence as readers and writers.

As the literature-based activities increased in JoAnn's classroom, the room environment took on a different look and tone as well. Print is every where: many books and displays about books, science and social studies realia sprinkled with books and student-made signs and posters, student mailboxes for interclass exchange of notes, graphs based on student polls and information gathering, sign-up sheets and schedules for classroom activities. These are but a few of the many kinds of functional print objects found in this classroom. JoAnn likes to refer to it as a language and literacy center.

Characteristics of an Effective Literature-based Program

A number of basic conditions must be met to ensure a successful literature-based curriculum:

Plenty of books are available throughout the school. Students have access to an abundance of books in their classroom library, the school library media center, and the public library. A plentiful and accessible resource of literature, selected with consideration for the age/grade range and topical interests of the students to be served, is essential.

In one school the library media specialist and the teachers had built an excellent collection of trade books related to the science and social studies units generally taught at each grade level. Finding good informational books at a broad range of reading levels had been a persistent problem. The problem was exacerbated when teachers moved toward theme-centered, literature-based instruction across the curriculum. By asking teachers to list the themes they anticipated teaching and sharing the compiled list with the entire faculty, the school library media specialist was able to enlist everyone's help in locating useful titles for the collection.

Literary study is an important part of the language arts program. At times several activities may focus on a single work of literature, a particular genre, or the work of a certain author or illustrator. Children have in-depth explorations into literature to extend their sense of story and develop a better appreciation and understanding of a body of literary work. In Dobbs Ferry, New York, a primary class undertook an intensive study of Leo Lionni's work. Over a period of two weeks, the teacher read his books on a daily basis and left them on display for the children to browse through at their leisure. She also researched and shared information about Lionni that went beyond the brief blurbs on the book jackets. Even these very young children were able to take a close look at the body of work to compare storyline, characters, and art. They talked about likenesses and differences in the books and their own preferences. The students began to understand that these lovely books originated in the mind of a creative person and that, as readers, they could look and talk about them with a critical eye.

There are opportunities for varied response to literature. Students use a variety of means to react to literary works. Responses may be written or oral, formal or informal, and make use of a variety of media. Opportunities for response should be offered during the reading of a book as well as at the completion of it. A fourth-grade teacher in New Jersey uses dialogue letters as one means of response to literature. After reading the first chapter or the first few pages of a book (whichever seems appropriate), children write the teacher a letter about their thoughts. Another letter is written when the book has been read. The teacher replies to each letter. The written dialogue allows student and teacher to reflect on the written work and to relate it to their personal lives as well as to other literary experiences. (See figure 9.)

The use of literature is evident across the curriculum. A literature-based curriculum should not be seen as something confined to the language arts program. Literature is an important resource in the study of any aspect of the curriculum. While it is frequently used in conjunction with textbooks, it is never viewed as supplementary to them; rather, it is one of the many important resources used to explore a theme or topic. An integrated literature approach to a science unit is shown as figure 10. A primary-grade teacher in Fairfax County, Virginia, makes extensive use of literature in a center approach to teaching science and social studies. Each center contains a large number of trade books on a topic and suggested activities involving reading and writing.

The library media center is an integral part of literacy activities for the entire school. Joint planning among administrators, teachers, and the library media specialist is essential for a successful literature-based program. Effective programs include well-prepared, full-time staff in the library media center as well as the classroom. The principal in one elementary school took her plea directly to the Board of Education, requesting that they restore the library and library media specialist to full-time status in

Dialogue Letters

Donna Carrera, a fourth grade teacher in New Jersey, reaches for a letter in a folder on her desk. She reads:

Dear Mrs. Carrara
   I like my book because it is weird and funny also its got a little mystery. The lead wasn't really pulling me in but I still wanted to read it. What I think is going to happen is Milo finds the Mathemagician It's about a boy whom isn't that smart and one day he gets a package which doesn't say where it's from and then he gets into another time zone. The arthur is Norton Juster and the title is the Phanton Tollbooth. I love the book it's great.

            from,

               Jimmy

She takes a clean sheet of paper and responds:

Dear Jimmy,

   I was very surprised that the lead didn't pull you in. What did make you want to read the book?
   The author seems to be saying that Milo must assume responsibility for learning. It's interesting how authors have messages in their books.
   I got the feeling that Milo entered another world as well as a time zone. Authors seem to be fascinated with this topic. A wrinkle in Time - The Chronicles of Narnia are just a few of these types of books.
   I'll be anxious to hear if Milo finds the Mathe- magician.
   I sense the author uses a little of the fairy tale element in this book. What do you think?

            Mrs Carrera

Reprinted from "Literature: Key Element in the Language and Reading Program" by Dorothy S. Strickland in *Children's Literature in the Reading Program*, ed. Bernice E. Cullinan (Newark, Del.: International Reading Assn., 1987), 69.

Figure 9. Example of Dialogue Letters

A Web of Activities

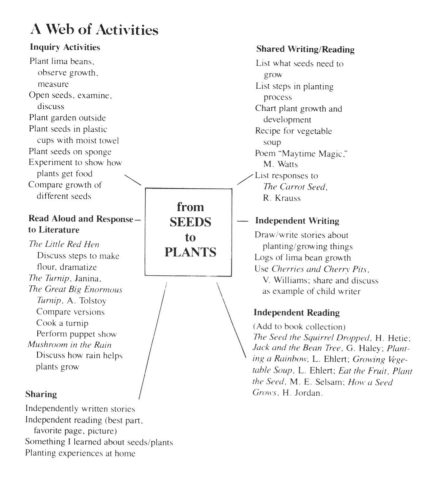

Inquiry Activities

Plant lima beans,
  observe growth,
  measure
Open seeds, examine,
  discuss
Plant garden outside
Plant seeds in plastic
  cups with moist towel
Plant seeds on sponge
Experiment to show how
  plants get food
Compare growth of
  different seeds

**Read Aloud and Response
to Literature**

The Little Red Hen
  Discuss steps to make
  flour, dramatize
The Turnip, Janina,
*The Great Big Enormous
  Turnip*, A. Tolstoy
  Compare versions
  Cook a turnip
  Perform puppet show
Mushroom in the Rain
  Discuss how rain helps
  plants grow

Sharing

Independently written stories
Independent reading (best part,
  favorite page, picture)
Something I learned about seeds/plants
Planting experiences at home

Shared Writing/Reading

List what seeds need to
  grow
List steps in planting
  process
Chart plant growth and
  development
Recipe for vegetable
  soup
Poem "Maytime Magic,"
  M. Watts
List responses to
  The Carrot Seed,
  R. Krauss

Independent Writing

Draw/write stories about
  planting/growing things
Logs of lima bean growth
Use *Cherries and Cherry Pits*,
  V. Williams; share and discuss
  as example of child writer

Independent Reading

(Add to book collection)
The Seed the Squirrel Dropped, H. Hetie;
Jack and the Bean Tree, G. Haley; *Planting a Rainbow*, L. Ehlert; *Growing Vegetable Soup*, L. Ehlert; *Eat the Fruit, Plant
the Seed*, M. E. Selsam; *How a Seed
Grows*, H. Jordan.

[center box:] **from SEEDS to PLANTS**

Reprinted from *Emerging Literacy: Young Children Learn to Read and Write* (Newark, Del.: International Reading Assn., 1989), 142.

Figure 10. Literature-based Activities in the Science Area

light of their critical roles in a literature-based curriculum. Budgetary cutbacks had taken their toll on the library media center, which is sometimes regarded as an ancillary part of the instructional program at the elementary level. Teachers made lists of the kinds of activities that were being curtailed because of the limited library support. The case was made for a well-supported library media center with a full-time, certified library media specialist. Moreover, the centrality of the library media program as the instructional core of the school curriculum was established.

Literature is used to link reading and writing. A conscious effort is made to link reading and writing throughout the instructional program. Lessons during writing workshops may feature examples from literature and discussions of the writer's craft. Students may discuss how authors develop plot, create good leads and closings, and use interesting language. They are encouraged to read like writers and to draw upon what they learn through reading as they attempt to improve their own writing. One teacher read aloud leads from three stories in the basal reader series used in the fourth-grade classroom. Each was written by a well-known author and was a good example of how good writers draw in their readers. The children then were encouraged to find similar examples in their independent reading to share with the group and to strive for interesting leads as they wrote their own stories.

There is time to read. Time must be set aside daily for independent reading in school. Self-selected reading should not be relegated to a mere example of an activity that may be done when students complete their other (and seemingly more important) work. Nor should it merely be offered as a homework assignment. It is valued as an important activity of each day. Independent reading must be given status. Documentation of independent reading is important. Students are more apt to take their reading more seriously if they have an opportunity to share their experiences with others. This sharing may be as informal as a brief sharing time at the end of each session, during which volunteers or students selected by the teacher share highlights or reactions to what they have read. Students may keep a daily log with brief entries regarding the titles they have read and discuss them periodically with the teacher. Kept diligently, the log can serve as a useful profile of each student as a reader. It can provide insight into individual preferences and reading trends that no standardized test can reveal.

Children are read aloud to daily. Participating in read-aloud sessions with opportunities to interact during and after the reading should be a regular part of each day's activities. Literature also can be shared through a variety of other media. Films, video and audio tapes, filmstrips, recordings, live drama, and storytelling are all viable ways to bring literature into the lives of children. Repeated readings of the same work and opportunities to experience it through various media help learners experience the piece more deeply and strengthen their understanding.

In a New York City school a teacher reads aloud to her children daily. After the reading she frequently gives the children a prompt for discussion in small response groups. For example, one day after reading "The Three Billy Goats Gruff," during which the children were adamantly pro–billy goat, she asked them, "Pretend that you are the Troll. How would you like it if those billy goats kept trapping over your favorite bridge?" Group leaders were chosen and the children scattered around the room for discussion. It was interesting to see how the children shifted point of view in favor of the Troll during their small group discussion. Later, the children returned to the whole group, and the group leaders shared what had been discussed. The teacher helped them to see how they had changed their perspective. Obviously, techniques such as this can be used at any level from the most elementary folk tales to Shakespeare.

Adults model their personal interest and pleasure in reading. Teachers and library media specialists share their reading with students and make conscious attempts to help students see them as readers. Adults as well as students read during independent reading time. A second-grade teacher in New York City participates in a literature sharing group that meets once a month at her home. In addition to reading and discussing adult contemporary novels, individuals sometimes share their writing. This teacher's second graders are aware that she is part of an adult response group much like those they participate in at school. She sometimes takes the book her group is currently reading to school and may even read a brief passage that is within the children's conceptual understanding. She recently shared the same piece of personal writing with her class and with her response group. The piece was about a time when her mother was extremely ill. In her writing, the teacher described her attempts to get her mother to the hospital and to see her through her illness. In contrasting the response from students and adults, the teacher found that her second graders sometimes ask questions that are as insightful as those of the adults and that their comments on aspects of the writing reveal a growing sensitivity to the power of language. Equally important, these opportunities help her students to see her as both a writer and a reader—much like themselves.

What Are We Trying to Achieve?

The most fundamental question in curriculum development is, "What is worthy of knowing and doing?" The growing body of research discussed in chapter 1 has caused educators involved in language and literacy to rethink the answer to this question. One compelling aspect of the research reviewed is that it draws on a diversity of disciplines, including psycholinguistics, sociolinguistics, anthropology, child development, cognitive psychology, and education. It stresses the social and functional nature of language learning and the active participation of the learner. It suggests instructional methods that promote the integration of all the language processes—listening, speaking, reading, and writing—and their interdependence with thinking and learning. Perhaps most important, these new understandings help to extend and confirm many important ideas that have been with us for a very long time. Significant among these is the role of literature in support of language and literacy.

Widespread interest in the use of literature as the foundation for instruction in the language arts and as a major resource throughout the curriculum has never been greater. Increased interest has important implications for the materials and methods used in the classroom and in the linkages between the classroom and the library media center. Goals such as those listed below, once found on the periphery of a school's objectives for reading, are now becoming central to the instructional program.

In summary, a literature-based curriculum seeks to help students:

- develop positive, skilled lifelong reading habits
- recognize, analyze, interpret, and evaluate literary works
- use literature to gain insight into themselves and others
- use literature to inform and build background knowledge in areas of personal interest
- increase their understandings of our culturally diverse, pluralistic heritage
- foster language growth and provide models of writing
- gain familiarity with literary forms and conventions as a means of appreciating, responding, and generating their own literature

Literacy instruction is in transition. The changes that are taking place are both encouraging and challenging. Teachers are encouraged by the prospect that their students will become better readers and writers and that they will make reading and writing something they choose to do. Many teachers and library media specialists are also experiencing a new sense of professionalism as they move, some slowly and some with great vigor, toward new ways of teaching.

Notes

1. Charlotte S. Huck et al., "Planning the Literature Program," *Children's Literature in the Elementary School*, 4th ed. (New York: Holt, Rinehart and Winston, 1987), 666–672.
2. *Handbook for Planning an Effective Literature Program, Kindergarten through Grade Twelve* (Sacramento, Calif.: California State Department of Education, 1987), 3.
3. *Handbook*, 3.

The Library Media Specialist's Contribution

The School as a Community of Learners

Teaching and learning strategies required by a literature-based approach involve changing roles for children and adults alike. Teachers traditionally have been perceived by students as completely in charge of learning in their role of knowledge-dispensers. On the other hand, teachers also have been perceived by colleagues, administrators, and many textbook publishers as slaves to the textbook. In the new scenario they become learners, too, as students of their own reading and writing process and as facilitators of learning for children. They have much to learn from each other and from the children they teach.

> I think integrated language arts works best when there is a team of teachers who work well together, because I think you really need to share. You really do need to find out a different way of doing something that worked well and could even work better. And I think we are going to have happier students. I think we are going to have students who are more vocal and more able to express themselves without difficulty.[1]

Thanks to research on early language acquisition, it is now understood that children are active learners, that they have an innate capacity and a powerful drive to make sense of their environments. Under the right circumstances they can become teachers of each other and of their teachers.

When information is pooled and shared among mixed-ability and mixed-age participants in cooperative peer group discussion, traditional patterns of control are altered by new ideas and attitudes about shared responsibility for learning. Teachers who establish these new relationships in their classrooms can no longer be perceived as slaves either to their own traditional leadership role or to any textbook or teaching method. They have, in fact, taken greater professional responsibility for being managers of their learning environments. Administrators who support these changes know that the evaluation processes for people and programs must be revised and expanded to acknowledge the greater complexity of the teaching/learning situation.

Teachers, administrators, and library media specialists who have accepted that shift in responsibility know how frightening the first steps can be. In most cases they must let go of familiar props and routines associated with lockstep instruction. Furthermore, they must become acquainted with an enormous wealth of materials. "It's more difficult to teach a literature-based, integrated curriculum because it's not materials-driven. It means that the teacher is the manager of the learning environment and is empowered to choose what materials to use and how to use them."[2] Empowerment inevitably translates into more responsibility and, therefore, more work. There is, understandably, an enormous amount of ambivalence about this change. "It used to be, maybe teachers were embarrassed because they didn't know about a book or, at the other extreme, embarrassed to be an expert on children's books. If you are someone who spends lots of time with children's books, you hesitate to let people know because they might think you waste time."[3]

In a time of uncertainty and ferment library media specialists have unique opportunities to forge strong partnerships with others in the school, sharing with them the hazards and the excitement of change. The three roles—information specialist, teacher, and instructional consultant—as described in *Information Power: Guidelines for School Library Media Programs*, must be mobilized to support the gradual implementation of a literature-based literacy program. But while the library media specialist's knowledge of children's literature is vital, it is important to emphasize the peer group connection with teachers as well as the expertise. Everyone is in this adventure together. Everyone must be involved in any professional development activity that calls for taking risks through writing. Library media specialists can be initiating activities that support pupil self-selection of books and written responses to literature, as well as activities that model various instructional strategies being implemented in classrooms. They can be planning and team teaching with colleagues both in the library media center and in classrooms. The opportunities and challenges are almost unlimited.

Establishing Partnerships: Signs of Progress

Many of the studies cited in the first chapter mention libraries only briefly, if at all. Although the literacy research agenda must be expanded to recognize the contributions of school library media programs, there has been increasing evidence that more practitioners are beginning to appreciate these contributions at the grassroots and state levels. The 1987 California Reading Initiative called national attention to literature-based literacy programs. The *English-Language Arts Framework*, published by the California Department of Education, makes a strong case for school library media programs. "Good libraries in the classroom, school, and community must accompany improvements in the English-language arts curriculum. . . . Every school must have its own collection of library media resources, including a variety of nonprint materials such as computer software, video cassettes, and audio cassettes. But just as important as the well-stocked and well-managed collection of books and nonprint materials is the librarian who encourages the use of these resources. As a part of the instructional team, librarians help teachers, administrators, and specialists select appropriate instructional materials. Librarians also teach students reference skills and guide them in selecting books and other materials to broaden their horizons."[4]

There are also examples of library-teaching partnerships reported by practitioners in Australia and New Zealand, where educators like Don Holdaway were among the first to develop many concepts and curriculum content for literature-based literacy programs.[5] A number of contributors to *Literature-based Reading Programs at Work* are teacher-librarians working in Australian and New Zealand schools.[6] One contributor to the work presents a ten-week library-based reading/writing program that was planned and taught with a third-grade classroom teacher. Another librarian describes her collaboration with a seventh-grade teacher to implement literature-based units organized thematically with topics drawn from social studies curricula. While most of these types of projects will be familiar to practitioners, the fact that they appear in an anthology of this kind is significant. Another author describes her two-year effort to introduce literature-based reading to classrooms in her elementary school in Elizabeth, Australia. "My approach has been a somewhat oblique one, but, I feel, appropriate to the circumstances. As a teacher-librarian I am not in a position of authority. I therefore had two tasks—to encourage change from within people themselves and to establish my own credibility as a program innovator."[7] This statement must have a familiar ring to many American library media specialists and reading specialists. It is a brief and clear statement of one individual's commitment to enacting the instructional consultant role "without portfolio." This proactive stance is probably the most successful way to implement this role and manage the balancing act with teaching and materials provision.

In a study entitled *When Writers Read* Jane Hansen describes a librarian who is a vital part of a community of readers and writers.[8] One has to read between the lines to get an idea of how the library media specialist may have functioned before the changes in reading instruction were implemented, but it is clear that library media programs have had a history of support in this community. The library media specialist has an assistant; that fact and flexible scheduling have always enabled the library media center to be open to students at any time of day. In addition she has very few scheduled classes; information skills instruction is based on teachers' and students' needs and is integrated with classroom curricula.

In the Hansen study the three roles of the library media specialist are implicitly understood in the author's description of a person who has "an overview of the school." The library media specialist is perceived as knowing the collection, knowing what's going on in every classroom, and knowing what children and teachers are reading and writing schoolwide. Among her scheduled classes are two regular weekly periods when children from every classroom (grades K–5) may participate in a response session, sharing with children from other grades the books they have either written or read. There is also a special area of the library media center dedicated to the children's own writings.

Perhaps the most important finding of the study is the increased use of the library by individual teachers. They search for children's books to read to their classes, to share with individual classes, to read themselves. Whereas they used to ask the library media specialist for guidance and recommendations for titles, now they are just as likely to share some insights about a favorite book or discuss a writing project that is giving them trouble. This change is seen in students as well, who are encouraged to share their responses to books they have read or those they are trying to select.

Teachers, library media specialists, and administrators have also been involved in the writing process as part of the school's professional development program. As members of a collaborative peer teaching and learning group, their knowledge of cooperative learning is based on first-hand experiences. They understand the frustrations, challenges, and strengths of this method of organizing classroom learning. Thus, adults and children in a community of learners see themselves as readers and writers, authors of literary works. As such, they have an "insider's" view of authorship; they see books as holding the contents of other people's minds and take a personal interest in interpretation. In this milieu everyone in the school has learned how to book talk or, rather, talk about books.

This study and others like it do not contain the final word on excellence in literacy instruction, nor do they offer prescriptions for the roles of participants in the process. Changes take place over time, and they are interactive. Participants in innovative programs must come to understand the nature and purpose of proposed changes, and they must internalize the goals and objectives. They must adapt to new circumstances and simultaneously begin to modify the innovations as they integrate them into their basic professional agendas.

> It's important for the teachers and librarians to work together—for us to plan units together, so that the teachers will use them as well as the librarians. . . . literature is not just the domain of the librarian, but it's to be used in all the classrooms.[9]

This observation was made by a library media specialist working in an elementary school in Monterey, California. She found herself developing new professional partnerships with colleagues as a result of the California Reading Initiative. Observers in other schools where literature-based literacy programs are being implemented report the same phenomenon. Members of the school community are working together in new ways in an atmosphere of excitement, optimism, and struggle.

Classroom teachers often have ambivalent feelings and relatively limited knowledge about resources and strategies for using children's literature. Many teachers are branching out from textbooks and seeking literature for all the content areas. They are eager for help. School library media specialists can take advantage of this opportunity to become teaching partners and instructional consultants, facilitators of children's and teachers' learning through collaborative planning.

Literature-based literacy programs rest on a firm foundation of resources and require an extensive knowledge of children's trade books and nonprint media, both informational and imaginative. In their role as information specialists, school library media professionals must build strong collections in all the content areas. Such collections are an indispensable part of resource-based teaching in elementary schools all over the country. Children in literature-based literacy programs must learn how to choose appropriate material from this wide variety of resources. Library media specialists help children to learn the information skills they need to locate, select, use, evaluate, and enjoy informational and imaginative literature.

Professional partnerships are important in initiating programs and in keeping them growing. Participants in healthy programs inspire and energize one another; they share expertise and ideas. Unfortunately, many elementary schools do not have either up-to-date library media collections or a qualified library media specialist running the library media program. In some schools the library media specialist works part-time or as a cluster teacher providing whole-group coverage for colleagues' preparation periods. School leaders who are developing literature- and resource-based literacy programs in the nation's schools must demand high-quality library media programs with ample resources, flexible scheduling, full-time professionals and clerical support, and strong connections with classroom curricula.

This demand will not materialize automatically. School library media professionals must take the initiative and step forward when they first hear the magic words "emergent literacy," "literature-based reading," "process writing," "writing to read," or any other terms to indicate that a shift in language arts instruction may be desirable or even imminent. Colleagues need to be reminded that the library media program can contribute both resources and expertise to any new curriculum initiatives.

By the same token, teachers and reading or language arts specialists must take the lead in promoting the development of good library media programs. Literature-based literacy programs call for collaborative relationships that break down traditional barriers created through the Balkanization of educational specializations so prevalent in large school systems. Language arts specialists and library media specialists must become natural allies in enabling teachers, students, administrators, and parents to realize their dreams of literacy for all children.

Validating Partnerships through Collaborative Inquiry

Once practitioners begin to implement a literature-based literacy program, how do they know it's working? What are the evaluative processes? Classroom teachers are used to having their efforts evaluated through formal assessment of their teaching by a supervisor and through formal assessment of pupil outcomes by means of standardized tests. In recent years teachers and library media specialists who are experimenting with new programs have been encouraged to assess student progress and their own learning by observing and recording classroom transactions on a regular basis. There is a healthy "trend to replace the researcher/teacher concept with a totally new one of the teacher researcher. Outside researchers no longer invade classrooms with preconceived notions of what should be done; teachers assume leadership as the professionals they are."[10] The motivation for this work includes the desire to improve one's own teaching as well as students' learning and to become more aware of successful practice by documenting it in detail. Some of this work may be done with outside consultants or educational researchers as part of a formal project. Much of the recent research on writing process and the relationship between reading and writing is based on such collaborations.[11] Some action research may be undertaken independently within the classroom or library media center; much may be done in collaboration with others in the school or district.

Cullinan and Strickland describe four approaches for observing, organizing, and analyzing data:

1. Select some aspect of language and literacy development and observe its development in all children;
2. Select certain children to observe in all or certain aspects of language and literacy development;
3. Structure a learning situation to observe children's responses and development over time;
4. Select a certain task or learning situation and vary it in specific ways in order to determine differences in response and development over time.[12]

Findings from such studies may be shared with a supervisor or a colleague in a conference, with members of the school community in a meeting, or in writing, even in a journal article.[13]

Library media specialists could collaborate with teachers in such efforts, and also may consider creating their own action research projects to document the effect of some aspect of the library media program on students' literacy development and learning. The first step in research often arises from a combination of confusion and curiosity. For example, a literature-based language arts program has been introduced and implemented in the middle grades for a year. Classroom teachers in the fifth and sixth grades make sure that they and their students get plenty of time to work with the library media specialist and the collection. Circulation of library materials to individual students in the fifth grade has nearly doubled, but it has actually diminished for the sixth grade. The researcher-practitioner asks, "What's going on here?" The answer may best be found through systematic data gathering and analysis in collaboration with the classroom teachers and students.

Curiosity may also arise from a sense of conviction and the desire for more certainty about a process that seems successful. The library media specialist has completed a genre study of selected picture books with a group of bilingual sixth graders with low reading scores. A definite improvement has been noted in the awareness of text structures, comprehension skills, and general confidence. The teacher reports that the students' written classroom compositions have also increased in number and shown unexpected improvement during and after the picture book study. She and the language arts specialist are urging that the unit be given at other grade levels and with mixed-ability groups. The researcher-practitioner is pleased but hesitant. Even success can have its downside. "I know the unit went well. But could I do it again? Why did it work so well this time?" The posing of this particular question should set the direction of study when the library media specialist repeats this unit with another group. Reflection leads to research.

There are a number of natural research questions for library media specialists to consider as a matter of program interest. One might be to ask how different ways of sharing stories with students affects their sense of story structure or story recall and comprehension. Do they remember more about the story if it is read aloud from a book? Told as a story event? Do they comprehend more if the follow-up activity is a class discussion? A dramatization?

Another approach might be a study of children's capacity for empathy with characters by analyzing discussions, retellings, or dramatizations of stories read aloud or together. Still another could relate students' recall and comprehension of various self-chosen texts to the text grammar or structure as categorized in standard story schemas.[14] What types of text seem most appealing? What types are most readily assimilated?

One well-traveled research path is an analysis of students' reading and viewing interests. Although there is a substantial literature in this area, there is always more to be learned as each new generation of youngsters interacts with many different kinds of communication media.[15]

There are a number of reading interest research models that can be adapted by practitioners: studies of library circulation; structured interviews; forced-choice questionnaires; reader-generated logs, journals, diaries of responses; and reading interest inventories, in which a ranking system is used to rate the level of reader/viewer interest in categories of titles arranged by genre and/or topic. Some of the reader variables selected in such studies include sex, age, developmental stage, intelligence quotient, reading ability, and attitude or motivation. Variables related to content can include age and sex of protagonist, setting, plot, genre, and theme or topic. Institutional or cultural variables can include availability of materials, socio-economic level and ethnic backgrounds of student population, parents' backgrounds and values, teachers' backgrounds and attitudes, and peer relationships.

Some practitioners like to begin with an informal general-interest inventory that can break the ice with a student and allow the library media specialist to get a sense of concerns and interests, to get a profile of the students behind the assignments.

There are a number of ways to organize such a survey. One approach is through a written questionnaire, which may be given to students during a scheduled period in the library media center. Data from such a questionnaire can be categorized and then either hand tallied or entered into a microcomputer database to compare the answers of, for example, students from different grades, from different classes in the same grade, from boys and girls in the same or different grade levels.[16] Figure 11 is typical of this type of questionnaire.

Another possibility for library media specialist collaboration is a reader response study. Many library media specialists have a good deal of experience with children's informal responses to literature and often comment on the difference between adults' and children's perceptions of some aspect of literature.[17] Such a study might best be conducted with a classroom teacher who is ready to or has already introduced literature response groups in the classroom. In such a curriculum unit small work groups of children are formed by the teacher to choose and read a book together, chapter by chapter. Data-gathering efforts may be focused on observations and field notes, teacher logs, student journals, audio- and/or videotape transcriptions of discussions among students, among students and teachers, and between teachers and researchers. "One of the most important outcomes of collaborative classroom research is the opportunity it gives teachers (and library media specialists) to systematically examine the instructional environment. They reflect on their discoveries both as independent learners and as members of a team sharing similar interests."[18]

Natural Roles, New Opportunities for Partnership

It is often said that curriculum changes, like changes in fashion, come and go in cycles. Most practitioners, however, view literature-based instruction as a basic, rather than cosmetic, shift in method and content. Literacy is both a fundamental goal of the education process and one of the primary conditions for learning in all school subject areas.

Current trends in reading instruction reinforce many of the traditional goals and objectives of school library media professionals: for example, there is more emphasis on comprehension skills and less on decoding skills; less dependency on textbook programs and more individualized reading and research in all the content areas; and the use of literature as integral to, rather than as enrichment of, the language arts program.

The importance of library media collections, programs, and professionals is being acknowledged in the efforts to improve education. Library media specialists must seize the opportunity offered by the renewed concern with literacy to exercise leadership and engender support in their schools. In order to promote literacy and the enjoyment of reading, library media professionals must consider the following questions:

What relationship should the library media specialist have with the reading specialist and the classroom teacher in regard to fostering literacy and reading comprehension in students?

How does the library media specialist contribute to planning and implementing the language arts program? What is the decision-making process for choosing programs and materials, and who is involved?

What special contributions do the library media specialist and program make to the student's development of advanced comprehension abilities?

What special contributions do the library media specialist and program make to the student's acquaintance with and understanding of literature?

How do the library media specialist and program foster in students the "library habit," and encourage independent reading for pleasure and information?[19]

WHAT INTERESTS YOU?

Name: _____

Room: _____

1. This is a list of popular types of TV programs and films. Underline the categories you like best and list a couple of your favorite TV programs or films in each category.

   a. Family Comedy

   b. Mystery/Adventure

   c. Horror

   d. Drama/Romance

   e. News/Documentaries

   f. Science Fiction

   g. Cartoons

   h. Game Shows

   i. Sports

   j. Other

2. Sometimes the commercials are more interesting than the shows. What are your favorite commercials?

3. If you were an actor or actress on television, what kind of parts would you want to play?

4. What are some programs that everybody in the family watches and enjoys?

5. What movies have you seen with other family members lately?

6. What magazines are usually lying around your house?

7. What magazines do you like to read?

8. What newspapers are you familiar with?

9. What parts of the newspaper do you enjoy most?

10. Has anybody in your family told or read stories aloud to you? If so, who, and what were the stories about?

11. What book are you reading for pleasure right now? (Give title and author, if possible.)

12. Where did you get it? Why did you pick it?

13. How do you choose a pleasure reading book? What qualities are important to you when you look for a book in the library, classroom or bookstore? (length? size of print? number of pages? story line? main character? etc.)

Adapted from "Changing Tastes in Children's Reading," by Eleanor R. Kulleseid in *Dimensions of Language Experience*, ed. Charlotte B. Winsor (New York: Agathon Press, 1975), 127-139. Reprinted with permission of Agathon Press.

Figure 11. Sample Questionnaire, "What interests you?"

14. Which would you rather read? Choose one out of each group of three and circle the number.
    A. 1—a science fiction adventure about an imaginary space flight to Saturn.
       2—a book describing the latest Apollo moon shot.
       3—a book of information about the solar system.
    B. 1—a book about life in a modern African country.
       2—a book about the history of the great African kingdoms.
       3—a book of African folk tales.
    C. 1—a book of games and puzzles.
       2—a book of jokes and riddles.
       3—a book of magic tricks.
    D. 1—a book of modern poetry.
       2—a book of modern short stories.
       3—a book of modern plays.
    E. 1—a book about human anatomy and reproduction.
       2—a book about the human mind.
       3—a book about animal behavior.
    F. 1—a book about medieval knights and armour.
       2—a book about everyday life in medieval times.
       3—a noel about a young person your age who went on the Crusades.
    G. 1—a book of horror tales.
       2—a good detective story.
       3—a science fiction novel.
    H. 1—a book of simple experiments with electricity.
       2—a book about the life of Thomas Alva Edison.
       3—a book about some young people who make a time machine and travel
          back to. . . .
    I. 1—a book about the adventures of a family.
       2—a book about the adventures of someone making his way in the world
          alone.
       3—a book about the adventures of a group of friends.
    J. 1—a sports fiction novel.
       2—a book on how to play football.
       3—a biography of Joe Namath.
    K. 1—a book about women's liberation.
       2—a book about Black Power.
       3—a book about student protest in colleges and high schools.
    L. 1—a book about relationships between boys and girls.
       2—a book about relationships between parents and children.
       3—a book about relationships between people and animals.

15. What real person would you want to read a book about?

16. If you were an author, what would your books be about?

Figure 11 (cont.) Sample Questionnaire, "What interests you?"

These questions are being explored by library media specialists, teachers, and administrators as new literature-based curricula are introduced and implemented. Some tentative answers are suggested in this volume. Meanwhile, many practitioners are reporting increased communication and cooperation. For example, the principal of an elementary school in Fairfax County, Virginia, believes that her school's new interrelated language arts program is on track partly because the essential and ongoing staff development process has been led by a team of internal change agents. They consist of the principal, the library media specialist, the reading teacher, a primary-grade teacher, and an upper-grade teacher. The process is described through a reference to a classic children's book. "We were taking a big risk, a long trip, and we had to figure out what baggage we were going to take along with us, and who was going to play which role as we went along our trip. The analogy I drew for the staff was that we were like the little engine that could. We were just going to barely make it out of the roundhouse, and going to have to figure out how far we have to go, and what steps we have to take, and we were continually saying to ourselves, 'I think I can, I think I can.'"[20]

Teams of change agents like the one described above are often created in response to district or state mandates but, once formed, have enormous influence on the fate of the project. Library media specialists must participate as vital members of these teams. Educational leaders are turning to library media specialists not only for their expertise in materials selection and use, but also because of their knowledge and love of literature. They serve as models for fellow teachers as well as students.

The vignettes presented in this book and in the video program *Literature, Literacy, and Learning* show professionals in various stages of the change process. Role concepts vary, notions of good teaching vary, and concepts of good literacy programs vary. What these educators hold in common is a dedication to experimentation, to taking necessary risks, and to changing their ways of teaching literacy so that children are empowered to take their rightful places in society. Such cooperative endeavors will enable teachers, library media specialists, administrators, and students in each school to see themselves as a community of learners whose words—spoken and written—are valued contributions to the human conversation.

Notes

1. Francie Alexander, interviewed during production of video *Literature, Literacy, and Learning*.

2. Alexander.

3. Jane Hansen, "The Librarian," *When Writers Read* (Portsmouth, N.H.: Heinemenn, 1987), 169.

4. English-Language Arts Curriculum Framework and Criteria Committee, *English-Language Arts Framework for California Public Schools, Kindergarten through Grade Twelve* (Sacramento: California State Education Department, 1987), 38–39.

5. Don Holdaway, *The Foundations of Literacy* (Sydney, Australia: Ashton-Scholastic, 1979).

6. Joelie Hancock and Susan Hill, eds., *Literature-based Reading Programs at Work* (Portsmouth, N.H.: Heinemann, 1987).

7. Hancock and Hill, *Literature-based Reading Programs*, 42.

8. Hansen, *When Writers Read*, 167–175.

9. Jane Evans interviewed during production of video *Literature, Literacy, and Learning*.

10. Bernice E. Cullinan and Dorothy S. Strickland, "The Early Years: Language, Literature and Literacy in Classroom Research," *The Reading Teacher* 39 (April 1986): 798–799.

11. See Donald Graves, *Writing: Teachers and Children at Work* (Portsmouth, N.H.: Heinemann, 1983) and Hansen, *When Writers Read* for two examples of projects conducted as

collaborations between classroom teachers and researchers from the University of New Hampshire.

12. Cullinan and Strickland, "The Early Years," 804.

13. For the report on a study of middle graders jointly conducted by library media specialists in three neighboring elementary schools, see John E. Bennett and Priscilla Bennett, "What's So Funny? Action Research and Bibliography of Humorous Children's Books—1975–80," *The Reading Teacher* 35 (May 1982): 924–927.

14. See Arthur N. Applebee, "Narrative Form," *The Child's Concept of Story: Ages Two to Seventeen* (Chicago: University of Chicago Press, 1978), 55–72; Brian Sutton-Smith et al., Introduction, *The Folkstories of Children* (Philadelphia: University of Pennsylvania Press, 1981), 1–43.

15. Alan C. Purves and Richard Beach, *Literature and the Reader: Research in Response to Literature, Reading Interests, and the Teaching of Literature* (Urbana, Ill.: National Council of Teachers of English, 1972) is a landmark study. See "ERIC/RCS: Children's Reading Interests," *The Reading Teacher* 37 (November 1983): 184–187, for a summary of more recent research. See also Ken L. Dulin, "Assessing Reading Interests of Elementary and Middle School Students," *Developing Active Readers: Ideas for Parents, Teachers, and Librarians*, ed. Dianne L. Monson and DayAnn K. McClenathan (Newark, Del.: International Reading Association, 1979), 2–15; Donald R. Gallo, "Are Kids Reading or Aren't They?" in "Library Connections," ed. Patsy R. Scales for *The ALAN Review* 12 (Winter 1985): 46–50.

16. For discussion of a microcomputer database of children's voluntary reading, see Linda Greengrass, "Creating a Database with Children," *School Library Journal* 31 (May 1985): 143–146.

17. See Arthur N. Applebee, "Fantasy and Distancing," *The Child's Concept of Story*, 73–85, for discussion of children's perceptions of fantasy and reality in stories.

18. Dorothy S. Strickland et al., "Research Currents: Classroom Dialogue during Literature Response Groups," *Language Arts* 66 (February 1989): 199. See also Dorothy S. Strickland, "Teacher as Researcher: Toward the Extended Professional," *Language Arts* 65 (December 1988): 764–774.

19. American Association of School Librarians and Association for Educational Communications and Technology, *Information Power: Guidelines for School Library Media Programs* (Chicago: American Library Association; Washington, D.C.: Association for Educational Communications and Technology, 1988): 7f.

20. Susan Warner, principal, Churchill Road School, Fairfax City, Virginia, interviewed during production of video *Literature, Literacy, and Learning*.

A Viewer's Guide to "Literature, Literacy, and Learning" Video

This viewer's guide presents ideas for using the video and book at faculty meetings, school meetings, for staff development, and parent-teacher programs. The purpose of this viewer's guide is to give some suggestions on how to use the video to accomplish the results that are important to you.

Description of the Video

Literature, Literacy and Learning is a 20-minute video for use by library media specialists, reading specialists and classroom teachers. The video presents new and revitalized approaches to language arts—whole language, integrated language arts, literature-based curriculum—and presents the key principles and characteristics that are common to each approach. The growing trend in literacy instruction is shown through many classroom examples in which the teachers capitalize on the integrated nature of the language arts and their relationship to the study of literature.

Narrated by Dr. Dorothy Strickland, Teachers College, Columbia University, the video shows examples of how literature is the springboard for reading, writing, speaking and thinking activities in elementary school classrooms.

> How does one recognize a school or classroom where there is teaching of integrated language arts across the curriculum? At first glance, through books. Everywhere. Students read; teachers read. They read quietly; they read aloud. Alone and in pairs. Not just for moments, but for dedicated blocks of time. Classrooms may be super quiet, or they may come alive with the sounds of reading. Library media centers become as familiar to students as their classrooms. Teachers and library media specialists become partners in a new and exciting way.
>
> Dr. Dorothy Strickland
> *Literature, Literacy and Learning* video

Using the Viewer's Guide

Option 1—View video as a whole

    A. **Overview:** Establish the purpose of the video prior to viewing the video. Give overview. Ask viewers to think about the five general questions that are provided in this guide.

The video is produced in conjunction with this book by Encyclopaedia Britannica Educational Corporation (© 1990, no. 4594).

  B. **After viewing:** Guide the discussion—return to the questions for discussion. Use other questions as desired.

  C. **Extend and apply:** Select from the list of activities given in this guide. Add others as appropriate.

Option 2—View video in segments

  A. First view the entire video without stopping.

  B. Prior to viewing the video the second time, establish the purpose of the video. Tell viewers that the video presents a number of schools where language-learning principles are in place. These classrooms and media centers have certain characteristics: these characteristics are provided below, along with some discussion questions pertaining to the segments on the tape. Each segment should be viewed and discussed separately. After viewing the tape in segments, ask the viewers to think about questions. (Note: music is used to divide the video into segments.)

  C. Select activities from the list.

Overview

Several different terms have been used to describe renewed approaches to teaching language arts. The goals and activities of these approaches—whole language, integrated language arts, and literature-based curriculum—are essentially the same. Perhaps the most basic of all is simply an appreciation of reading and writing and a love of literature in all forms.

The basic message of the renewed approach to language is to get the students into the work by integrating listening/reading, writing and listening activities. Literary works are emphasized and the organizer is the book.

The video provides some models for how this approach looks in the classroom and the media center. It also shows how the teacher, library media specialist and reading/language arts specialist can work together to make this happen in the instructional program.

Questions for Segment on Listening and Speaking

Language learning is an active process and a social process in the classroom. In the video, there are students who are discussing things, sharing their knowledge, sharing their ideas. They are not passive learners being force-fed information. They are actively engaged in the process.

- Language learning is an active process and a social process. How is this shown in the video?
- All language learning involves the construction of meaning. What examples are given that show effective use of purposeful reading and writing?
- What is the role of the basal text? Is there a de-emphasis on breakdown of skills?

Questions for Segment on Reading

There is an emphasis on children's literature and a de-emphasis on worksheets.

- What are some creative ways that big books are used?
- What examples are given of discussion groups and student response groups?

- Can you suggest other cooperative learning approaches?
- How are publishing centers used?
- What is the relevance of literature to the goals of teaching? How do teachers help each other in implementing the approaches suggested in the video?

Questions for Segment on Writing and Assessment

The classroom provides a print-rich environment (abundance of books, magazines, visuals) that helps students actively engage in their own writing. The process of learning is emphasized, not the product.

- What examples are shown of how the teacher, media specialist and reading specialist work with students during the writing process?
- What creative writing approaches are presented?
- What illustrations are given of the stages of the writing process—prewriting, drafting and revising, publishing? What other examples can be shared from your own experience?

Assessment is an integral part of instruction. It is a process orientation rather than a product orientation.

- What examples are given of conferencing as an assessment tool?
- What scenes in the video show that cooperative learning is going on?
- Several approaches to assessment are included. Are they flexible and practical? Do you agree with these approaches?

Questions for Segment on Integrated Listening/Speaking/Reading/Writing

Language instruction is not fragmented. Language learning grows out of the learner's previous experience. It is pragmatic, functional and purposeful for students.

- How do the integrated approaches to language arts stretch the learning of students?
- How are large blocks of time scheduled for theme work, integrated work, and long-term work?

Some General Questions

- As you view the video, notice how students use oral language to facilitate learning. Note and discuss how oral and written language are used effectively in support of one another.
- Observing good practice is both confirming and informative. Note at least one practice given in the video that you already use in your classroom and one that you would like to try.
- Dealing with diversity is a challenge for all teachers. Note ways in which students function at different levels and in different ways within the same classroom.

Examples of Possible Group Activities

- With a partner, generate a list of creative ways that library media specialists and classroom teachers can work together to support a literature-based language arts program.
- What are ways of keeping up with the new literature being published?
- What are ways of getting more literature into the classroom and library?
- What are ways of organizing the classroom and the library to facilitate a literature-based program?
- How can you organize and manage literature response groups on these issues:
  - a) independent, self-selection or common book;
  - b) number of share sessions per week;
  - c) conduct of share sessions;
  - d) use of teacher prompts for reading;
  - e) methods of response beyond the share session;
  - f) projects.

Eleanor R. Kulleseid is director of library services at Bank Street College and teaches Language, Literature and Literacy at the Bank Street Graduate School. Kulleseid is the author of *Beyond Survival to Power for School Library Media Professionals* (Library Professional Publications, 1985); she holds a doctorate and master's in library science from Columbia University.

Dorothy S. Strickland is the Arthur I. Gates professor of education in the Teachers College at Columbia University. She holds a doctorate and master's degree in early childhood and elementary education, specializing in reading, from New York University. Her publications include *Emerging Literacy: Young Children Learn to Read and Write* (IRA, 1989).